A History Of The Presbytery Of Corisco, Ogove River, West Coast Of Africa

Robert Hamill Nassau

In the interest of creating a more extensive selection of rare historical book reprints, we have chosen to reproduce this title even though it may possibly have occasional imperfections such as missing and blurred pages, missing text, poor pictures, markings, dark backgrounds and other reproduction issues beyond our control. Because this work is culturally important, we have made it available as a part of our commitment to protecting, preserving and promoting the world's literature. Thank you for your understanding.

A HISTORY

OF THE

Presbytery of Corisco

Rev. R. H. Nassau.

Ogove River, West Coast of Africa,
February, 1888.

Trenton, N. J., U. S. A.:
From the Press of Albert Brandt, Jr.

1888.

CONTENTS.

	PAGE.
PRELUDE,	5
I. ORGANIZATION OF CORISCO PRESBYTERY,	6
II. ORGANIZATION AND GROWTH OF CHURCHES,	8
III. REDUCED MEMBERSHIP,	11
IV. UNUSUAL METHODS AND DISORDERLY ACTS,	12
V. DISCIPLINE,	14
VI. CHURCH WORK,	15
VII. CANDIDATES FOR THE MINISTRY,	17
VIII. SYSTEMATIC BENEFICENCE AND SELF-HELP,	20
IX. PASTORSHIPS AND SUPPLIES,	21
X. CATECHUMEN INQUIRY CLASS,	22
XI. REVIVALS,	23
XII. WOMEN'S WORK,	23
XIII. ROLL OF MINISTERS,	24
XIV. MODERATORS,	25
XV. LIST OF STATED CLERKS,	26
XVI. NECROLOGY,	26
XVII. PRESENT STATISTICS,	27
XVIII. THE OUTLOOK,	28

A HISTORY

OF THE

Presbytery of Corisco.

PRELUDE.

A MISSION of the Board of Foreign Missions of the Presbyterian Church in the United States of America, was located on Corisco Island, in Corisco Bay, Bight of Benin, Gulf of Guinea, equatorial west coast of Africa, in June–July, 1850, by the Rev. Messrs. James L. Mackey and George W. Simpson and their wives.

Mrs. Mackey died suddenly in May, at Gaboon, before the actual location had been decided on, (the new Missionaries being temporarily guests of the adjacent A. B. C. F. M. Gaboon Mission).

Mr. and Mrs. Simpson were drowned from a small vessel, in a tornado, off Fernando Po Island, within a year after the location.

Mr. Mackey, left thus entirely alone, was subsequently joined by, in 1852, Rev. George McQueen; in 1853, Rev. Messrs. Edwin T. Williams, William Clemens, and their wives; in 1855, Rev. Cornelius and Mrs. De Heer; in 1857, Rev. Thomas Spencer and Mrs. Ogden; in 1859, Chauncey L. Loomis, M.D., and Mrs. Loomis; and at intervals by several unmarried ladies, the Misses Isabel

Sweeny, Caroline Kaufman, Maria M. Jackson, and Georgiana M. Bliss.

The first Station was built at Evangasimba, on the western side of the island. Subsequently two other Stations were added—Ugobi, two miles distant toward the southern end, and Elongo, three miles distant on the northern end.

With changes from marriages, deaths and removals, there were present in the Mission in May, 1860, Rev. J. L. and Mrs. Isabel Mackey, Rev. Wm. and Mrs. Clemens, Rev. C. De Heer, Rev. T. S. and Mrs. Ogden, Dr. C. L. and Mrs. Loomis, and Miss Jackson.

One Church had been formed, at Evangasimba, in 1856.

I. ORGANIZATION OF CORISCO PRESBYTERY.

FROM this point begins the history of Corisco Presbytery. On May 7th, 1860, almost exactly ten years from the Mission's first establishment, "in accordance with previous notice, after due consultation had, there were convened at Evangasimba, Rev. James L. Mackey, Rev. William Clemens, Rev. Cornelius De Heer, Rev. Thomas S. Ogden, and C. L. Loomis, M.D., missionaries laboring at the three Stations on Corisco Island, viz., Evangasimba, Ugobi and Elongo, together with the three native Elders, Andĕke, Ibia and Ubĕngi, (of whom Andĕke represented the Church,) for the purpose of forming a Presbytery. The opening sermon, from the words, 'O Lord, my God, thou art very great,' Ps. 104:1, was delivered by Rev. J. L. Mackey, the oldest Minister present."

Mr. Mackey was elected Moderator, and Mr. Clemens

Temporary Clerk. After the organization, Dr. Loomis and the Rev. Walter H. Clark were invited to sit as corresponding members. The former was immediately appointed Stated Clerk; and the latter was, at a subsequent meeting, placed on the Examining Committee.

Dr. Loomis was an Elder in a Church in America, had studied Theology at Union Seminary, New York, was licensed by a Missouri Presbytery, but had not with him his certificate. Mr. Clark had transferred himself to our Mission from the A. B. C. F. M. Gaboon Mission, and was laboring in our bounds, but had not yet received his formal appointment by the Presbyterian Board, nor his certificate of dismissal from his Presbytery of North River.

Presbytery's name was officially "Corisco," and it was voted to connect with the Synod of New Jersey. This selection was had, probably, through the interest of the brethren in the fact of their loved Theological Seminary being in Synod's bounds. But only one, Mr. Ogden, belonged to that Synod (Presbytery of New Brunswick); Messrs. Mackey, Clemens and De Heer belonging to, respectively, Chester, Pa., Washington, Pa., and Wooster, O.

The new Presbytery was cordially accepted by Synod, at the hands of delegate Mackey, during his visit to America in 1860–61; and that fact was reported by him, on his return, to Presbytery, at its meeting, October 19th, 1861.

II. ORGANIZATION AND GROWTH OF CHURCHES.

1. CORISCO CHURCH.

THE mother Church of the Presbytery was formed in 1856, the first Communion being held on October 1st, of that year, on which occasion Ibia and Andĕke were baptized, and at first was called "Evangasimba"—afterwards changed to "Corisco." It grew from crystallization of the first native converts around the ladies of the Mission and a few Christian Liberian servants who accompanied the pioneers. In the beginning, before there was material for native Eldership, the ordained missionaries exercised the functions of both Teaching and Ruling Elders. Even after a board of native Elders had been obtained, the original clerical members of that Church, and some of their successors on Corisco Island, sat and voted in the Evangasimba Church Session—a practice which sometimes was attended with evils. It has existed in none of the other Churches, except the Gaboon, where it was allowed to an unnecessarily late day.

2. BENITA CHURCH,

Fifty-three miles north of Corisco. As comity to the A. B. C. F. M. Gaboon Mission limited growth southward, and inter-tribal jealousies barred advance eastward toward the interior, Church extension went northward. Pupils to Rev. W. Clemens' Elongo Mainland School came from Benita and Batanga; Scripture-readers were sent to the Benita and Bata districts; Rev. George Paull, in January, 1865, began the erection of the Mbâde house, Benita. At a meeting of Presbytery, April 11th, 1865, authority was given for the organization of the Benita

Church. But Mr. Paull's lamented death delayed the act. It was not consummated until December 11th, 1865, when a Committee of Presbytery (Rev. R. H. Nassau and Ruling Elders Ibia and Njumba) erected a Church of eighteen members, including Elder Njumba, of the Corisco Church, all of whom lived north of Cape St. John. That Elder was never regularly installed over the Benita Church. As the new Church was set off by direction of Presbytery—not at the request of the Church members themselves—and as it was constituted of *only* the set-off eighteen Corisco members (and none others) over whom already that Elder had been installed, the Committee supposed that the episcopal action of Presbytery rendered unnecessary an additional installation ceremony.

3. GABOON CHURCH.

When the Gaboon Mission of the A. B. C. F. M. was transferred in 1870 to our Presbyterian Board, and by it merged into our Corisco Mission, the Congregationalist Society, existing since 1843, at Gaboon, was, by direction of Presbytery, through Committee (Rev. Messrs. Bushnell and Gillespie), June 14th, 1871, re-organized as a Presbyterian Church, and on their report, August 19th, 1871, enrolled the third on our list of Churches.

4. BATANGA CHURCH.

Seventy-five miles north of Benita. The establishment of the Batanga Church was by order of Presbytery, in precisely the same way—with much of the same reasons, and with a Ruling Elder as one of the colonizing company—as in the case of the Benita Church. The order was made in meeting of January 13th, 1879, erecting into a separate body all Benita Church members living north of Evune. The actual organization, as reported by the Committee (Rev. Messrs. Ibia and Murphy), was made April 16th, 1879, with "thirty-eight members set off from Benita Church, with Itongolo, and two others newly elected, as Elders."

5. OGOVE CHURCH,

One hundred and sixty-five miles up Ogove River, at Kângue Station. A written request to Presbytery, "signed by four members of Gaboon Church and two of Benita Church, residing permanently in the Ogove," was granted at meeting of July 21st, 1879. The organization by Committee (Rev. R. H. Nassau), was effected November 28th, 1879, with those six applicants, and H. M. Bacheler, M.D., medical Missionary, who offered his certificate of membership from the Summit Presbyterian Church, New Jersey, and who accepted the office of Ruling Elder, to which he was immediately regularly elected, ordained, and installed. At a meeting of Session, next day, ten candidates for baptism were examined, of whom three were received. Five of those six who signed the request to Presbytery were the first Ogove converts, and they had been taken to the sea-coast Churches for baptism.

6. EVUNE CHURCH,

About forty miles north of Benita. The second colony from the fruitful Benita Church was the Evune, set off in May, 1881, with twenty-one members, without, as far as appears from the records, any request to or authority from Presbytery. Rev. C. De Heer, at its meeting December 14th, 1881, reported that he had organized such a Church; "and, on motion, it was enrolled, and its Elder, Mbai, admitted to a seat."

7. "FIRST PRESBYTERIAN CHURCH OF BATA,"

About twenty miles north of Benita, the third Benita colony, was, at the written request of Benita Church members, authorized at the meeting of Presbytery, January, 12th, 1883, and subsequently organized by Committee (Rev. Messrs. Gault and De Heer, and Elders Ebuma and Etiyani), on September 25th, 1883, by setting off forty-one members, "baptizing one new member on profession of her faith, electing two Elders and installing them both, first having ordained one, the other having been an Elder in the Benita Church."

III. REDUCED MEMBERSHIP.

PRESBYTERY, organized with only four clerical members, has never had less than three to continue its organic life; but, several times, by the absence of one or more of its members in America, it has been without a working quorum. Shortly after its organization, Mr. Mackey left, on a visit to America, the three other members remaining on the ground. It is recorded that one of them, Rev. C. De Heer, in order to make a quorum at the meeting of April 9th, 1861, was brought into the Church, sick with fever, "wrapped in a blanket and laid on a pallet."

During all of 1864, and again for a whole year in 1870–71, there were no meetings, there being only two members on the ground.

On June 25th, 1880, a meeting is recorded as constituted with Elder Bacheler as Moderator, and only two

Ministers (Messrs. De Heer and Truman), the certificate of a new member (Rev. A. W. Marling) being subsequently received during the sessions.

And on January 7th, 1884, another meeting is recorded with only two members (Rev. Messrs. Nassau and Gault) actually present; a third (Rev. W. H. Robinson) lying in an adjacent house, too sick to be moved; and a fourth (Rev. A. C. Good) arriving after the meeting was adjourned.

Indeed, the *final* reason for the ordination of Licentiate Ibia, on April 5th, 1870, was for the salvation of the Presbytery's organic life—the expected absence of Mr. De Heer and dismissal of Mr. Menaul, leaving only Mr. Nassau actually on the ground. The same final reason prevailed to the ordination of Licentiate Truman, on January 7th, 1880, the expected absence of Mr. Nassau and dismissal of Mr. Murphy, leaving only Mr. Ibia actually on the ground.

IV. UNUSUAL METHODS AND DISORDERLY ACTS.

THIS occasionally reduced membership led to some unusual, and perhaps unpresbyterial, methods.

1. At the meeting October 19th, 1861, Mr. Clemens about to be absent in America, the two remaining members (Rev. Messrs. Mackey and De Heer), were appointed an "Executive Committee with power *ad interim*." Subsequently, October 10th, 1865, the circumstances being similar, it was voted that whenever the Presbytery should be reduced, by absence in America, to less than a quorum, the remaining two members on the ground should be an *Ad Interim* Committee, " who shall continue in office one year and until discharged by Presbytery, whose duty it

shall be (1) to receive credentials of applicants for admission to Presbytery, and make examination according to Presbyterial usage; and when they shall approve such men, they shall report their names to the Stated Clerk, who shall enroll them in the Book of Records; and such applicants shall be then considered regular members of this Presbytery. (2) The said Committee shall also be authorized to examine candidates for the ministry on their studies when they are prepared for such examination. (3) It may also examine Sessional Records. The acts of this Committee shall be submitted to Presbytery for approval at the next regular meeting, or whenever Presbytery shall call for their report." Of the above-named vested powers, the second (2) was never exercised. The Committee's (Rev. Messrs. Mackey and De Heer) first act was, about December, 1861, to receive the credentials of Rev. R. H. Nassau, from the Presbytery of New Brunswick, who, *ipso facto*, became a member of the Presbytery, and a constituting member of the meeting of January 18th, 1862, that received the credentials of Rev. Walter H. Clark, from the Presbytery of North River. The Committee's (Rev. Messrs. Nassau and Ibia) last recorded act is the reception and recording of the name of Rev. Albert Bushnell, D.D., from the Presbytery of Cincinnati, on June 14th, 1871; since which time, the occasional difficulty (notwithstanding our increased membership) in obtaining a quorum, has not been caused by " absences in America;" and, therefore, the Committee ceased to exist.

2. During all of 1860, Dr. C. L. Loomis acted as Temporary Clerk, at each meeting being invited to sit as " corresponding member," and being elected Stated Clerk for the year, though he never had any regular connection with Presbytery. And, in 1861, Rev. Messrs. Clark and Nassau, sitting as corresponding members, were placed

on Committees, and spoke and acted in all respects (except voting) as if full members.

3. A Stated Meeting was held June 25th, 1880, by only two Ministers, receiving during its sessions the credentials of a third, and enrolling as a representative Elder, a native who never was an Elder. The Presbytery, thus constituted, proceeded to deprive of licensure a native brother, for an alleged offense which an informal (and therefore unrecorded) investigation by Presbytery, six months previously, had decided did not call for discipline; and appointed as Stated Supply of the Gaboon Church a Congregational Minister (laboring in the employ of Mission within the bounds of Presbytery, but having no connection with it other than corresponding membership), who, assuming possession of the Gaboon Church Books and Session, had dismissed to a distant point the native Minister whom Presbytery had regularly located as Supply over that Church. This state of affairs continued for more than two years, protested against by only one member of Presbytery; the other members, while admitting the illegality of the proceedings, excused the allowance of them by their personal respect for the Congregational brother, and the deference due to his talents and long-continued service in the Mission.

V. DISCIPLINE.

THE frequent changes and reductions in the membership of Presbytery, while they barely escaped destroying its organic life, did destroy its consistency, and made its discipline irregular and neglectful of recorded rule. New members sometimes failed to acquaint themselves with our historic precedents. A leaven of independency carried, at times, severity even to the point of despotism possible under Congregationalism, but which the bars and checks of faithfully-executed Presbyterianism so justly prevent. At other times, there was laxity that took no notice of what had previously been severely dealt with. The inability to maintain an invariable standard of opinion in a fluctuating membership, and the disregard of old rules by new members, led, at different times, to inconsistent positions and acts on even grave moral points. Native church members were, at times, disciplined for acts affecting the seventh Commandment, which, at other times, were passed by unrebuked; disciplined, at times, for acts regarding temperance and Sabbath observance, for which same acts even members of Presbytery went unchallenged.

VI. CHURCH WORK.

BUT if these preceding points, in a truthful and impartial history, must be recorded, we can speak with honorable pride of consistent, faithful and efficient work done through the evangelistic labor of Bible-readers. As early as the meeting October 19th, 1861, a Committee (Rev. Messrs. Clemens and Nassau and Dr. Loomis) " was authorized to bring before Presbytery, in such a form as they may see fit, the duty of Presbytery toward native helpers, especially as to their examination respecting their religious views, their motives on entering the work, the doctrines they hold, their general fitness for the work, and the appropriate manner of setting them apart for their employment." That Committee, "The Mainland Visiting," changed to two members, never for ten years lost its organic life, vacancies being regularly filled. Its field of operations lay from Cape Esterias on the south,—eastward in the Munda River and in the Bay at Ukâkâ, Hondo and Mbangue,—and northward at Cape St. John, Italamanga, Aje, Hanje, Upwanjo, Meduma, Bata, Batanga, and other intermediate points. It located Scripture-readers at most of those places, traveling hundreds of miles yearly in their inspection, encouragement and, sometimes, protection. As other fields were opened up, their prominent points were thus occupied by similar Committees. This is lately especially true in the Ogove River under Rev. A. C. Good, where the Bible-readers have been the strongest arm of the work. They have contributed largely to the recent in gatherings of the Church membership there. In the Benita region they were the pioneers of the three Churches colonized from the original Benita Church. They were from the first regarded as under the appointment, inspection and direction of the Presbytery; the Committee in charge being itself subject to Presbytery, making regular written reports, and its acts being open to criticism and alteration.

But at the meeting January 7th, 1884, a radical measure was passed, Presbytery abdicating all its right over and interest in the Bible-readers, leaving their selection, employment, wages and work, solely in the control of each individual Missionary within the bounds of his parish. There may be ground for question whether, in so doing, Presbytery did not neglect an important Church interest, the work itself be not in danger of losing its sacred character, and the workers themselves liable to take it up as they would any merely secular job. The plea for the change was that, as the Committees, by Presbytery's failing to fill vacancies, had ceased to exist, and the work had afterward been carried on by individuals in their separate parishes, those individuals should be allowed uncontrolled charge of their own work.

VII. CANDIDATES FOR THE MINISTRY.

ANOTHER most important duty that has ever claimed the attention of Presbytery was the inducting of worthy young men into the ministry; the native Church members being early charged that the support and propagation of the Gospel in their own country belonged to them, that it could not always continue an American import. To this end, the first missionaries, even before Presbytery was organized, each at his own Station, had carefully taught and encouraged their best pupils to seek the ministry. So that, at the very first meeting, May 7th, 1860, the three native Elders, Andĕke, Ibia and Ubĕngi, having already privately passed the necessary studies, under the tutelage and special patronage of respectively Rev. Messrs. Mackey, Clemens and De Heer, came for examination, and were assigned trials for licensure. At that same meeting, a Committee (Rev. T. S. Ogden and Dr. Loomis) were appointed to report a liberal course of study for future candidates. And, at the meeting January 9th, 1872, a Committee (Rev. Messrs. Gillespie and Bushnell) reported a still more extended course.

As the English is to our candidates a foreign language, proficiency in it was always accepted instead of Latin, Greek or Hebrew. Recently, also, meeting January 5th, 1886, the rule requiring even a knowledge of English as a pre-requisite for licensure, was relaxed in favor of certain native laborers, "who, by their exceptional zeal and success, had shown themselves worthy of the ministerial office." From the beginning, almost every Missionary, male and female, has had some favorite pupil or pupils whom their personal interest led into candidacy. So that the honor of raising candidates can be claimed solely by no one member of Mission or Presbytery. But these pupils often became discouraged and dropped out. The multifarious businesses that distract a Missionary's time and attention at each Station often made his teaching irregular, and the students turned aside, wearied at the delay on the way to the goal of licensure. These delays were increased by removals of the patron Missionary from the field. The successor could not always fully assume the role of patron to the (to him or her) comparatively unknown protege; misunderstandings and losses inevitably came, and the native helpers, with a hurt feeling against individuals, charged Presbytery as a body with lack of sympathy for them. However true this charge may have occasionally been, Presbytery made effort twice, in 1872 and in 1883, to relieve the evident discontent, by attemping to gather at the central Gaboon Station, students from all other Stations, into a proposed Theological Training School, under the special instruction of, successively, Rev. Messrs. Bushnell and Good. But the efforts were unsuccessful. Candidates now, as formerly, grow up where their tribal interests lie, or where their employment during part of each day as Station assistants affiliates them with the teacher of their own choice. Thus, any teacher in the Mission may have charge of one or more candidates. Presbytery has, several times, officially recognized the efficiency of their labor, particularly so that of Miss I. A. Nassau, who, longer than any other one person, has engaged herself in this special work. As a result of these various efforts to raise a native ministry, over the twenty-eight years of the Presbytery's life, there have been on our roll twenty-eight candidates, not including many others who were students to that end, but who dropped out before actual enrollment.

Of these twenty-eight, there have reached ordination three, viz., Rev. Messrs. Ibia, Truman and Myongo. Eight others (Andĕke, Owondo, Kongolo, Petiye, Mbora, Etiyani, Igui, Reading) reached licensure; four of them (Andĕke, Owondo, Petiye, Kongolo) went back to the world, but one of these (Owondo) afterward returned, entering his name again on the list of cadidates, thus leaving at present, licentiates, four. Of the remaining eighteen, one (Tongo) died in good standing. Dropped out, without discredit, five, (Uhemba, Ngâude, Melumur, Âkâ, and H. M. Bacheler, M.D.) Dropped with censure, five, (Ubĕngi, Bombanga, Ibolo, Ijabi, Komanandi.) Leaving on the roll at present, seven, (Owondo, Bapite, Eduma, Divine, Itongolo, Joaque and Ogula.)

RECAPITULATION.

Ordained,		3
Licentiates { Licensed,	8	
{ License revoked,	4	4
{ Restored as candidate,	1	3
Died in good standing,		1
Dropped, without censure,		5
Dropped, with censure,		5
On roll at present,		7
Total,		28

VIII. SYSTEMATIC BENEFICENCE AND SELF-HELP.

EVERY Pastor and Supply has, in his own way, and according to his degree of interest on the subject, urged the native Churches to self-support. But there has been no systematic plan. Natural covetousness has prevented the natives from making energetic effort. Indeed, those communities, *e. g.*, Gaboon, which—by the presence of white missionaries and the expenditure of foreign funds in building of houses, feeding and clothing of pupils, and employment of workmen—have received the largest amount of aid, have been the slowest to give for their own Church expenses. While those, *e. g.*, Batanga, which have been steadily refused the white man's expensive presence, and which, as a condition of our sending them even native teachers and preachers, were required themselves to build school-house, Church, &c., have responded the most abundantly. The Mission custom of providing EVERYTHING for the school children, food, clothing, washing, mending, books, lights, bedding, eating utensils, etc., etc., evoked no gratitude, seemed only to harden selfishness, until it was seen to be an evil. Then, meeting January 13th, 1879, the simple entering wedge of a change, *i. e.*, the requisition that at least books should be paid for, was complained against and resisted. But, finally, that requisition and a few others are in force.

One native brother, Rev. Ibia, as early as 1865, felt the evil habit growing on the aborigines, of depending for support on foreign missionaries and traders. He asked to be allowed to establish and receive temporary aid in a project at Mbangue, a point in Corisco Bay, which, he hoped, would eventually become self-supporting, where "everyone who will marry but one wife, and live industriously, is encouraged to come and live." Oil-palm, cacao and cocoanut trees were planted, in the hope of creating an honest trade, free from the dangers of the dishonest "trust system" in vogue on the coast. Carpentering also was taught, and the breeding of cattle and fowls for sale was tried. The enterprise was commenced, but, for various reasons, has not had the hoped-for results. Nevertheless, Mr. Ibia has since, in season and out of season, with a reformer's zeal, but with very little success, urged on his people the duty of casting off their inherited laziness; and has, sometimes, received therefor from them a reformer's painful isolation and even hatred.

IX. PASTORSHIPS AND SUPPLIES.

THE undesirable letters "S. S.," appear very frequently in Presbytery's annual statistics to Assembly. But they represent, not the American relation covered by the name "Supply," but the inevitable instability of our connection between preacher and people, due to our constantly fluctuating membership and frequent absences in America. It seemed undesirable to constitute a pastoral relation that was to be broken in a few years, or at least interrupted by absences of a year or two. It has resulted, therefore, that the Minister whom necessity or the Mission happened to employ at any particular Station, was appointed by Presbytery, without any reference to his fitness or the wishes of the people, "Stated Supply" of the Church gathered at that place. The only actual pastorships regularly formed on call from the people and installation by Presbytery, were: Over Corisco Church, Rev. J. L. Mackey, January, 1862, to June, 1865; and Rev. Ibia J'Ikĕngĕ, called in 1880, but not installed till February 7th, 1883. Over Benita Church, Rev. S. H. Murphy, 1872 and 1873. Over Gaboon Church, Rev. A. Bushnell, D.D., from 1872, till his death, in 1879.

Licentiates have constantly been used as Supplies, with a neighboring Minister to moderate Session and administer Sacraments.

X. CATECHUMEN INQUIRY CLASS.

PROFESSION of faith in Christ is not, in our field, the cross it is in many countries. It rarely has brought persecution. Indeed, Church connection often brings the obscure native into enviable prominence. Our Sessions are aware that baptism and the Christian name are sometimes sought, with only a perfunctory performance of public Christian duty, as a social distinction. A singular aspect of our work is therefore revealed, viz., that of *barring* the way to the table by a probationer's class, and by various delays of Session. A resolution of Presbytery requires all who ask for baptism, to first pass at least one year's instruction under the Minister, Licentiate or Bible-reader nearest to them, and to at once give a partial proof of their sincerity by complying with our rules as to polygamy, slave-holding, use of intoxicating liquor, and Christian marriage ceremony, and by making a faithful effort to learn to read the Bible in their own tongue.

XI. REVIVALS.

ALL parts of our field, each in its "accepted time," have been at intervals blessed with revival. The natural socially-sympathetic feelings of the Negro may often have been involved in the causes that drew the crowd; and too little has there been expression of tearful sorrow for sin, and earnest longing after righteousness. Too often there crop out in Session examinations desire of escape from the trouble sin brings as punishment only in this life, and a coveting of the benefits of civilization that accompany Christianity. But, with all this chaff, we believe much precious grain has been gathered for the garner. Latterly, especially in the Benita and Ogove districts.

XII. WOMEN'S WORK.

THE more silent, but often powerful influence of the work of foreign white (with a few native) Christian women, being under the government of the Mission, has not come under Presbytery's official charge or inspection, except in the cases of the female missionary teacher of candidates for the ministry, and of the few natives (notably among them Mrs. Benje-Itongolo, of Benita, and Mrs. Bessy Makae, of Gaboon,) who have labored as Scripture-readers. But, limited as has been Presbytery's direct or official connection with the patient toil of these and of other women, it would be an omission, in a historic sketch, not to acknowledge its value and success.

XIII. ROLL OF MINISTERS.

THE whole number of Ministers connected with the Presbytery, from its organization to February, 1888, is twenty-two (22), as follows:

1. Rev. James L. Mackey,* from Presbytery of Chester. Died. (See list of deaths.)
2. Rev. William Clemens,* from Presbytery of Washington. Died. (See list of deaths.)
3. Rev. Cornelius De Heer,* from Presbytery of Wooster.
4. Rev. Thomas Spencer Ogden,* from Presbytery of New Brunswick. Died. (See list of deaths.)
5. Rev. Robert Hamill Nassau, from Presbytery of New Brunswick. Received, 1861.
6. Rev. Walter H. Clark, from Presbytery of North River. Received, 1862. Returned to America. Dismissed to Presbytery in Nebraska, 1871.
7. Rev. George Paull, from Presbytery of Redstone. Received, 1865. Died. (See list of deaths.)
8. Rev. Solomon Reutlinger, from Presbytery of Winnebago. Received, 1867. Died. (See list of deaths.)
9. Rev. John Menaul, from Presbytery of North River. Received, 1868. Returned to America. Dismissed to Presbytery in Arizona, 1871.
10. Rev. Ibia J'Ikĕngĕ. Ordained, 1870.
11. Rev. Albert Bushnell, D.D., from Presbytery of Cincinnati. Received, 1871. Died. (See list of deaths.)
12. Rev. Samuel L. Gillespie, from Presbytery of Chillicothe. Received, 1871. Returned to America, 1874. Left without letter. Name dropped.

---

* Presbytery organized, 1860.

13. Rev. Samuel H. Murphy, from Presbytery of Chicago. Received, 1871. Returned to America, 1874. Left without letter. Name dropped. Came back from Presbytery of Winona, 1878. Returned to America, 1880. Dismissed to Presbytery of Mankato, 1881.
14. Rev. J. C. deB. Kops, from Presbytery of Chicago. Received, 1871. Returned to America, 1873. Left without letter. Name dropped.
15. Rev. Wilhelm Schorsch, from Presbytery of Chicago. Received, 1874. Returned to Germany. Insane. Name dropped, 1878.
16. Rev. Ntâkâ Truman. Ordained, 1880.
17. Rev. Arthur Wodéhouse Marling, from Presbytery of New Brunswick. Received, 1880.
18. Rev. Graham Cox Campbell, from Presbytery of St. Paul. Received, 1881. Returned to America. Dismissed to Presbytery of St. Paul, 1888.
19. Rev. William Chambers Gault, from Presbytery of Steubenville. Received, 1881.
20. Rev. William Harvey Robinson, from Presbytery of Kittanning. Received, 1881. Returned to America. Dismissed to Presbytery of Kittanning, 1887.
21. Rev. Adolphus Clemens Good, from Presbytery of Kittanning. Received, 1883.
22. Rev. Frank Sherrerd Myongo. Ordained, 1886.

XIV. MODERATORS.

THE roll of Moderators coincides so very closely with the above list of Ministers as to be almost a repetition of it. A spirit of impartiality in the distribution of office was seconded by our often limited material. A somewhat regular rotation has therefore brought into the Moderator's chair, in succession, at least once, every Minister, excepting Rev. Messrs. Truman, Myongo and George Paull, the latter of whom was connected with the Corisco Mission little over a year, and with Presbytery only four months. Rev. Messrs. Nassau, Bushnell and Gault have each held the chair two years, Rev. Ibia J'Ikĕngĕ three years, and Rev. C. De Heer seven years.

XV. LIST OF STATED CLERKS.

1860. Corresponding Member, Elder Licentiate Chauncey L. Loomis, M.D.
1861. Rev. James L. Mackey.
1865. Rev. Robert Hamill Nassau.
1873. Rev. Samuel Howell Murphy.
1875. Rev. Robert Hamill Nassau.
1880. Elder Henry Martyn Bacheler, M.D.
1881. Rev. Robert Hamill Nassau.

XVI. NECROLOGY.

There have died:
1. Rev. Thomas Spencer Ogden, May 12th, 1861, on Corisco Island, of African fever.
2. Rev. William Clemens, June 24th, 1862, at sea, on board ship en route to America, of yellow fever.
3. Rev. George Paull, May 14th, 1865, on Corisco Island, of African fever.

4. Rev. James L. Mackey, April 30th, 1867, at New London, Pa., U. S. A., of consumption.
5. Rev. Solomon Reutlinger, July 17th, 1869, at Mbâde, Benita, of erysipelas.
6. Rev. Albert Bushnell, D.D., December 2d, 1879, on board British mail steamer, harbor of Sierra Leone, W. C. A., of pneumonia.

XVII. PRESENT STATISTICS.

Ministers—9.	Churches.	Communicants.
Rev. Cornelius De Heer,	Benita, S. S.,	195
Rev. Robert Hamill Nassau.		
Rev. Ibia J'Iknĕgĕ,	Corisco, P.,	85
Rev. Ntâkâ Truman.		
Rev. Arthur Wodehouse Marling.		
Rev. Graham Cox Campbell (in trans.)		
Rev. William Chambers Gault.		
Rev. Adolphus Clemens Good,	Ogove, S. S.,	91
Rev. Frank Sherrerd Myongo,	Batanga, S. S.,	128
Licentiates—4.		
Spencer Trask Mbora.		
Etiyani,	Bata, S. S.,	113
George William Bain Igui.		
Joseph Hankinson Reading,	Gaboon, S. S.,	45
	Evune, V.,	90
Candidates—7.	7	747

XVIII. THE OUTLOOK.

IN the beginning of the year 1887 the problem faced us, viz., What to do with all the Churches, communicants, and the work connected therewith in the Gaboon and Ogove parishes? the Presbyterian Foreign Board having advised the Mission to retire to the northern and German part of our field, and transfer to the Protestant Church of France, all the work, including two of our Churches, lying in French Colonial territory. To part with those Churches would have been like giving away a hand or an eye. But the transfer, it was hoped, would be for the aid and better protection of our Church members living under French government. Now, however, with this history brought up to February, 1888, that painful problem has been partially solved by that French body's financial inability to accept the proposed transfer, but by showing their willingness to aid us, in furnishing, at our Board's expense, French Protestant teachers. By their presence we will be able to comply with the education requisitions of the French government, and will hope to have removed some of the restrictions that have hampered educational and other work in our bounds.

Printed by Libri Plureos GmbH in Hamburg, Germany